Words for a Dazzling Firmament

Poems/Readings on Bereishit Through Shemot

Abe Mezrich

Ben Yehuda Press
Teaneck, New Jersey

Published by Ben Yehuda Press
122 Ayers Court #1B
Teaneck, NJ 07666

http://www.BenYehudaPress.com

To subscribe to our monthly book club and support independent Jewish publishing, visit https://www.patreon.com/BenYehudaPress

Jewish Poetry Project #24   **http://jpoetry.us**

Ben Yehuda Press books may be purchased at a discount by synagogues, book clubs, and other institutions buying in bulk. For information, please email markets@BenYehudaPress.com

ISBN13 978-1-953829-19-1

22 23 24/ 10 9 8 7 6 5 4 3 2 1   20220829

Contents

The Story of Freedom 🐇 Shemot Through Mishpatim

Words for a Dazzling Firmament

Poems/Readings on
Bereshit Through Shemot

Abe Mezrich

Notes on Translation, Transliteration, and the Names of God

1. *The translations throughout this book are mostly my own, with help from the Jewish Publication Society (JPS) Tanakh when I wasn't sure how best to render a word or phrase into English.*

2. *I have not always been consistent with how I transliterate Hebrew words, and how I refer to the various names of God, from poem to poem.*

3. *There are many ways to express the truth.*

–AM

Here is the Story

The beginning of Torah is the story of how God made
a cosmos and humanity and a family and a people.

This book is a book of thoughts about that story.

And what must we people do with this story?
We must use it to guide us
from a family to humanity to the cosmos
and up to God.

Abe Mezrich

The Beginning

The Book of Bereishit

Abe Mezrich

Bereishit

There is No Warrior

God sets angels to guard the Tree of Life,
so we will not eat from it
as we ate of the Tree of Knowledge.

In a different story, a warrior might
outwit the angel & live forever.
But not here.

Instead, this:
Our own choice put the angel there, put life beyond us.

_____

Genesis 2:22 - 24

Abe Mezrich

When You Lose, You See

i
The first time he learns he is a thing of dust
is when God punishes him.
He and the woman eat the fruit
and God says:
Now you must work the earth
I made you from
until you return to dust

for you are dust,
and to dust you shall return.

ii
He had been the center.
It was he who gave the animals names
who named woman *Woman*
because she came from *man,*
from him.

Now he names her Eve,
Chava:
for she will be
the mother of all life.

iii
If you lose everything,
you can know new things:

How if you have lost so much
perhaps it was never you
who held the universe.

How if you were first
perhaps it was only to ready the way.

How a man is a mere piece of ground
here to care for the soil.

You will be ready
for what you must do next:

to give others
their rightful names,

to reach for the earth—
not to take,
but to tend.

————

Genesis 3:19-20

Abe Mezrich

Incomplete

i
God makes Man from God's breath and soil,
from earth and sky.
He says: *It is not good for Man to be alone*
and makes the Man sleep
and fashions Woman from the Man's body.
The Man wakes to meet his wife.

*

Jacob flees his brother.
Stopping to sleep on the way,
Jacob dreams of a great ladder
running from earth to heaven and back.
When he wakes, he walks to where he will meet his wife.

*

Receding into their solitude,
the Man and Jacob make room
for Heaven on Earth,
and for God to send someone to fill the void.

ii
The mystics speak of how God contracts,
making space for the universe.

Maybe it is we who must cede space
to receive Him,
to encounter each other.

———

Genesis 2:18 – 23; 27:41 - 29

Abe Mezrich

Noach

What God Told Noah Before the Rain Fell

Where there are no men, strive to be a man.*
- Mishnah Avot 2:5.

Where there is no great one to hold the earth,
you must fill the emptiness;

sometimes all that stands against devastation
is you on a ship in the ocean
waiting for birds to fly back.

Now: take the Creation in two by twos
and hover above the rivers
over the mountains,
like revelation.

I will look away.

The birds are circling and circling
their feet aloft
and the world needs you:

you, the one
who must tend the drowned
and saved;

you, the living

——

Genesis 6-7

* *Translation based on Sefaria.*

In Noah's Ark

The animals come male and female
Noah's whole family comes

it is not enough to save all the creatures
to save the world

you must save togetherness
you must save love
or at least the possibility of love.

____

Genesis 6:19

Dove & Lamp

When the Flood ends,
Noah takes an olive leaf:
a gift from the dove.

In the Mishkan, we offer our own olive oil
to light the lamps
to light the darkness.

Survival receives,
holiness gives.

––––
Genesis 8:11; Exodus 27:20
I may have recalled the last line of this poem
from a poem I read elsewhere.

Taking Life

i
God tells the first man and the first woman:
I give you every herb and every tree to eat.
He does not mention
the eating of animals.

After the Flood,
God tells Noah:
Everything that crawls on the earth
is yours as food,
like the green herb.

ii
Only after the Flood could we eat meat.

iii
Before you bear responsibility for taking life
first you need to understand the destruction of a world.

————
Genesis 1:27-29, 9:1-4

Abe Mezrich

Lech Lecha

Where we Go

i
Where do the first people go?
There and back:

Adam and Eve
go *east of Eden*

& the people of Babel
migrate *from the east.*

There and back.

ii
Abraham enters the war:
four kings against five,
fighting in every direction,
Abraham rushes in
to rescue the captives.

Abraham who journeys South,
Abraham to whom God says
Look to the North, South, East, and West,
look to the sand and stars,
I give you the world
to make it blessed.

iii
What does Abraham care
for the axis people have travelled before
since the start of time?

There are captives in every direction.

Everywhere there is a world to save.

————

Genesis 3:28, 4:9-16, 11:2 - 4, 12:1-9, 13:14 - 14:20

Righteous Economy

i
Abraham flees to Egypt
from the famine in Canaan.

He fears the Egyptians will kill him
over his beautiful wife.

When there is not enough land
for Abraham and his nephew,
Lot,
their shepherds come to fighting.
They part ways.

This is what it is like
in a world of scarce things.
Fight or flee.

ii
In the war
Lot,
the people of Sodom,
the things the people possess
— they are all captured.

When Abraham rescues them
the king of Sodom says:
I will take the *souls*, the people;
you, Abraham, keep the property
you have rescued.

A payment:
people for things.

Abraham says:

You, king, keep everything—
the people
and the things that come with them.

iii
What you have
what can be taken from you

what can be captured
or killed or purchased
—all that can be taken away—

in a world of scarcity
we call that your worth.

iv
Abraham is not interested
in worth.
He knows a human soul is priceless.

He refuses to take away
the value of a man
from him.

————

Genesis Chapters 12 - 14

Learn to Fight

i
Abraham tells Sarah:
Pretend you are my sister
so they do not kill me over you.
Abraham tells Lot:
Brothers should not fight.
Leave me.

Abraham forgets the story
of Cain & Abel.

He thinks brothers and sisters
are the opposite of conflict.

ii
But Abraham's offspring will wrestle
until they find the truer way:

brothers at war,
then brothers who refuse to speak,
then a nation of brothers.

iii
Do not hide from the conflict.
Fight through the sacred tension
to the true togetherness.

____

Genesis Chapter 4, 12, 13

Abe Mezrich

You Have Not Come Back to Us Yet

the story of Lot

Do not say
you will be away forever.

I will tell you a story.

Once a man travelled with a saint
to the promised land.

He was the saint's nephew,
the saint's adopted son,

and he left behind his whole life:
the houses and trees and people he knew

and he followed the saint
to that new place.

But the nephew grew rich
and his workers and the saint's workers bickered.
And maybe it was not only the workers,
maybe the nephew
did not love the saint anymore.

After,
the nephew moved to a wicked city
and his daughters gave him so much wine
he did not know it was them
when he placed his own children
in their bellies.

Later one kingdom that grew

from one of those babies
sought out a prophet to curse
the saint's own children.

So yes,
he was away.

But then hundreds of years passed
and something else happened.
Another daughter
snuck back to the saint's kin.
Your people will be my people,
she said.
Your God will be mine.

She became
the great-grandmother of the king.

What I am saying is that the world is still young
and there is time to retrace the journey.

What I am saying is that you could still lead us
back to us.

What I am saying is remember please
how we used to walk:
in love, headed somewhere
in shared steps.

Genesis 12:5; 13; 19; Numbers 22 – 24; The Book of Ruth

Abe Mezrich

VaYeirah

Signs of Life

i
Where are you?
Ayekah?
God calls to the man & the woman
who are hiding from God in Eden.

Where
ayeih
is Sarah, your wife?
the angel asks Abraham
who stands outside the tent
that she is inside.

ii
Soon after the Man names the woman
Chavah / Eve:
from *chai—life,*
for she will be
the mother of all life.

Sarah is barren; but the angel says:
At this time next year,
Sarah will bear a son.

At this time next year,
but in Hebrew
כָּעֵת חַיָּה
in a time of life.

iii

Abe Mezrich

Ayekah?
Where are you?

You are next to the source of life
who sits beside you
but you did not see.

Seek them
as God seeks you.

—

Genesis 3:9, 20; 18:9-10

The One About the Woman and the Baby

There is another way of viewing the world.
Think of a joke,
the way a punchline in a joke reveals
that the story made sense all along
but only now at the very end you find out why.

Sarah is ninety.
She is an old woman.
Motherhood is for someone else,
not for her by now.
But God tells Sarah she will name her son Isaac
whose name means laughter.

Through Isaac she will birth a whole people
and become a matriarch
and she has been a matriarch this whole time
but she only learns this now, in her very old age.

When she learns this, she laughs.

Sometimes the punchline comes
and there is a reason for laughter.
The story always made sense
if you learn to hear it
the way God tells.

____
Genesis 17:1 – 18:16

Abe Mezrich

In Sodom We Believe So Much

The people of the city to Lot

Because from far away
you saw all the richness of this place
—luscious and full of green
like the Garden of Eden—

you left behind the saint
whose God gave light.

In Eden they ate the fruit
& their eyes were opened.

In this Eden
tonight we grabbed so fiercely
we all went blind.

Here we believe
taking is its own kind of creation.
We add our darkness
to the darkness.

————

*Inspired by Rabbi Elchanan Samet's reading of Genesis Chapter 14.
See also Genesis 1:3, 3:7, Chapter 19*

Mercy for the Wicked

God descends to Sodom & Gomorrah, hearing their *cry*.

Who cries? The people of the wicked cities.

So God hears even the cry of the wicked.

___

Genesis 18:17 – 19:13

Mother of Salt

all its soil devastated by sulfur and salt[1]
His wife looked back and turned into a pillar of salt[2]

seeing what she saw,
what else could she do
but what a mother does—

give her whole self
so something might rise?

salt was on that ground
but when she looked

salt grew tall
as a grown woman.

————
[1] *Deuteronomy 29:22*
[2] *Genesis 19:26*

after Lucille Clifton

How to Be Abraham

i
Leave your father's house, your homeland,
your nephew, your firstborn child.
Let them take your wife away (say: She is my sister).

Agree to slay your one remaining son.
Learn that no, God does not want that,
God never wanted that.

ii
The first test: See how many you can part from
in the name of the Journey.

The next test: See if you can keep them close,
if you can stay.

Genesis Chapter 12-13, 21:9-21, 22:1 - 15

Chayei Sarah

Fragility

i
When Adam sinned, he blamed Eve
and they were expelled from the Garden
to go to die.

ii
When Sarah died Abraham eulogized her—
which is to say: he explained her life.

Then he bought her a burial plot,
our first ancestral land in Israel.

iii
We sin and we die.
We are fragile.

Our fragility
is a fissure we can attack through
and through it we can uproot our whole world.

But our fragility is also a window
to understand another through.
Through that understanding
we hold fast to the earth,
forever.

———
Genesis Chapter 3, 23

Abe Mezrich

Interdependence

i
Abraham hopes for a wife for his son.
He sends his servant out to seek this wife.

ii
We do not know the servant's name.
When Abraham charges him with his task,
the servant is called *his servant, the elder of* Abraham's *house.*
When the servant meets Rebecca
—whom he will take to Abraham's son, Isaac, to marry—
he is called *the servant* and *the man.*

He has no identity of his own.
He is a conduit for those around him.

Because of him,
Abraham's small family
becomes many generations,
becomes a nation.

iii
This nation comes to be
through the man who has no self.

This nation comes to be
through the man who is only for others.

Only from such a man can a nation grow.

———

Genesis Chapter 24

The Chosen

i
Abraham's servant says: Let me drink from the water
you have drawn.

Rebecca says:
I will give to you
and I will give to your camels also.

So she fulfills the sign.

ii
Rebecca's family says: this is from God,
we will not hold her back,
but let her stay with us
just one more year.

The servant says: God has shown already
she is the one to come with us.
Let us go now.

And Rebecca's family says: Let the girl decide.
And Rebecca says: I choose to go now.

iii
Even the chosen ones
must choose themselves.

____

Genesis Chapter 24:1-58

Place

Returning from meditating in the field,
Isaac *lifted up his eyes and behold: camels were coming.*
Rebecca is on one of the camels.

She of the long journey,
he of the meditation in one place.

From their marriage, Israel comes.

———
Genesis 24:61-63
With Rabbi Yaacov Steinman's reading of
Genesis 24:61-67 as a jumping off point.

Abe Mezrich

Toldot

What We Do There

Why does God put
the man in the Garden?
To work it and to guard it,

to tend to the *plants of the field*
—**siach** ha'**sadeh.**

Isaac goes out *la'suach* ba'*sadeh*:
to pray in the field.

From the place of plants
and man's care—
prayer.

Maybe we reject Esau,
man of the field,
Isaac's beloved son,
because he is a *hunter.*
A hunter,
he undoes Creation.
So we reject him.

What do you do
with the Garden that God offers you?
You could tend.
You could pray.
You could hunt.

Choose.

Genesis 2:5-15, 24:63 (translation based on Rashi), 25:27

Abe Mezrich

This is What is Certain

i

One day Esau returns from the hunt
and he is starving.

It would seem that he has caught no food that day,
or not enough.

It is his brother Jacob,
cooking stew at home,
who feeds him.

The hunt is always uncertain.
Only the home life is certain.

ii

Isaac, their father, tells Esau:
Catch me something to eat...*that my soul may bless you.*

But it is Jacob who brings a dish first.

How did you find food so quickly?, Isaac asks.
Jacob says: I happened upon the catch
that God has sent me.

iii

Jacob's answer is not wholly true.
Jacob's mother prepared the dish herself
from the family flocks.

Jacob has called his mother's home-made dish
a wild catch that God has sent.

iv
But Jacob also says this
right before he is forced from home
into decades of turmoil.

So say Jacob has struck upon the real truth,
just in time:

even in our home we are like hunters,
waiting for the catch to come
and nothing is certain

and the only certainty
is the gift that God sends.

––––

Genesis 25:27-34, 27:1-20

Enemies

Esau is ruddy & craves Jacob's red stew.
Jacob wears fur to be hairy like Esau.

In our enemies
we seek ourselves.

———

Genesis 25:25-34, 27:1-22

Seekers

In Babel the people try to build a tower up to Heaven,
but God does not let them.

Isaac and his men do not build upward.
They dig wells in the earth.
And God blesses Isaac.
And Isaac and his men reach water.

Perhaps God does not want us to reach toward Heaven.
Perhaps He wants us to entrench ourselves in the earth,

in the place where we stand.
In the place where we live.

Our blessing is there.

———
Genesis Chapter 11, 26:13-25

VaYeitzeh

Where We Go

i

Jacob leaves his father's house to go to Paddan-Aram.
On his way he comes to *the place*.
The place is not named for us when Jacob arrives.
It is only *the place*.
*

Jacob falls asleep.
He dreams of a ladder.
The ladder's base is on the earth. Its top is in Heaven.
Angels of God ascend and descend upon it.
*

Here is the gate to Heaven, Jacob says.

ii

When you travel from place to place,
you are in no-man's land.
Your *place* has no name,
as Jacob's *place* has no name.
*

But traveling, you learn that you can arrive
at a place from somewhere else:
Paddan-Aram from your father's house.
*

From this knowledge, you can understand
how all directions are connected:
how above can be reached from below
how you can walk from Earth to Heaven.
You will see the tall ladder, spanning from Earth to Heaven.
You can see the creatures *ascend*ing and *descend*ing on it.

You will know you may be at the gate to Heaven right now,
wherever you are.

————

Based on the writings of Avivah Zornberg
Genesis 28:10 - 22

Abe Mezrich

Love

There are too many shepherds here
for Jacob to speak to Rachel alone.

They are waiting for more shepherds to come,
and then more shepherds.

Together they will move the enormous stone
that covers the well's mouth.
Then they will take the well's water and go.

But Jacob does not want to wait for more shepherds.
He wants to speak to Rachel right now,
when his heart needs her.

That is why he moves the enormous stone
himself,
with his own hands.

Now the shepherds can come and draw water
before they had ever hoped.

Sometimes love is so strong
it reaches past you
and provides for a world.

————
Genesis 29:1-11

Who Should Be King

i
On her sister's wedding night
Leah's father switches her sister with her
under the cover of darkness.
When her husband wakes up in the marriage bed,
it is Leah beside him.
That is how Leah is married to her husband
through her father's trick.

She names her first three sons, saying:
- *now my husband will love me.*
- *God has heard that I am hated,*
so *He has given me* another son.
- *Now my husband will join me:*
for I have birthed him three sons.

Her whole life is made
by a father
who sent her to the husband
who never wanted her.

ii
Her fourth son she names *Judah,*
Yehudah,
from the words *praise*
and the name of God.

This time
Leah says
I will Praise HaShem.

In the name Judah there is no husband
and there is no father.
There is a woman praising God.

Abe Mezrich

Judah sires the line of David,
the line of kings.

iii
Who should rule us?
Not the father who forces us into life.
Not the husband we implore to love us.
Only the one through whom we find our own voice
to praise God.

———
Based in part on Rav Amnon Bazak's writing on the Books of
Samuel
Genesis 29:18 – 25, 31-35

See

i
Jacob sleeps in a place.

Suddenly God appears to him in a dream.

Jacob says: *HaShem is in this place, and I did not know.*

*

Jacob is to marry Rachel.

But on *the evening* of their wedding, Lavan
—Rachel's father—
switches Rachel with her sister, Leah.

And it came to pass that in the morning, behold: it was Leah.

*

Jacob does not recognize the place of God.

He does not recognize the woman he marries
—the woman who names their first three sons
in the hope that he will finally see her.

Jacob is a man who does not see.

ii
Later Jacob grows wealthy. And Lavan
grows to mistrust him.

*And Jacob saw the face of Lavan; and
behold: it was not with him as before.*

*

Abe Mezrich

Jacob saw the face of Lavan.

Jacob has learned to see another person.

iii
It is then that God,
who has not spoken to Jacob for twenty years,
says to Jacob:
Return to the land of your fathers.

And Jacob journeys away.

And *angels met* Jacob.

And *Jacob saw* the angels
there, in the broad daylight.

And Jacob *said: This is God's camp.*

*

Jacob sees the face of another person.

In this he becomes able to see God's world.

————
Genesis 28:10 – 22; 29:22 – 25, 31-35; 32:1-3

Abe Mezrich

VaYishlach

What is Your Name

Jacob wrestles an angel. That angel changes Jacob's
name. The angel says strikes at Jacob's thigh. *Your name
will be Israel now,* the angel says. Jacob, who is now
named Israel, limps away. Because the angel has hurt
Israel in the sciatic nerve, *the Children of Israel do not
eat of the sciatic nerve* when they eat meat *to this day.*

Jacob was wounded once and *to this day* we
cannot stop being reminded of that pain and
making our pleasure a little bit less.

Our empathy must run so deep that it reaches back to the
first pains our people felt thousands of years before us.

Such great empathy comes to us with our very name.

_____

Genesis 32:25-33

Abe Mezrich

Perfect

Jacob, just named by the angel,
is damaged by the angel,
now he walks with a limp.

The angel, who has no name,
cannot win a battle
with a struggling man.

No one in this story is complete.

Everyone in this story is holy.

____

Genesis 32:25-33

Enemy

Jacob's leg is torn
on the eve of his break from Esau
his enemy
his brother
his twin.

Even an enemy
can be a part of you.

———

Genesis Chapter 32

Even a Flicker Matters

i
Cain's line dies out in the Flood
but we still learn the names of his descendants.

ii
Esau's descendants
are not part of Israel,
they are barely mentioned in the Torah.
But we learn the names of the patriarchs of Esau's family.

iii
Even if you are a story that does not go on
you still bear a name,
you still bear a meaning.

———

Genesis 4:17-26, 36

VaYeishev

Judah Discovers Togetherness

the woman with no face in the bed
is the woman who waits on the road

is the woman who never was
so they said to me

is the foreign woman
who hurt my sons
my good sons

is the woman who holds my cord,
my rope,
my ring

is the woman who holds my cruelty
the sting of it
tucked for years in her heart

is the woman who holds my lineage
right there in her belly

is the woman whose great-great-great grandson
will build the house of the Lord.

My house will be called a house of prayer
for all peoples
the prophet will say.

_____

Genesis 38; Isaiah 56:7

How We Find Freedom

i

Joseph is sent by his father to see his brothers as they tend
the *flocks*.

But Joseph's brothers hate him. When they see Joseph,
they throw him into a pit. They cast him from the
family. They leave him to the elements to die. And
they *sit down to eat bread*. And they *dip* Joseph's
garment in goat's blood. And he is brought down to
Egypt, to slavery. Later the whole family follows him
to become slaves for two hundred years and more.

ii

When God saves Israel from Egypt, He tells the
people to offer a lamb *of the flocks*. And to partake of
the lamb *by family*. And to eat the matzah, the bread
of memory. And to *dip* hyssop into the lamb's blood.

The first meal of freedom is Joseph's slavery in reverse.

> When the leper is healed, the priest dips hyssop
> into bird's blood and the healed one rejoins his
> people then. And he is not an outcast any more.

The first meal of freedom is the dip in hyssop.

Bring the outcast back in the family, and freedom comes.

Genesis 37; Exodus 12:1-22; Leviticus 14:1-32

*Note that the ceremony of the leper is introduced
significantly after the Exodus; however, I am assuming
a single set of symbols applied throughout the Torah.*

What do Dreams Mean?

i
Joseph is his father's favorite son
and his father gives him a special coat.
Joseph lives a charmed life.

At night Joseph dreams
and his dreams imply that his brothers will bow to him.
But Joseph is taken into slavery
and from slavery to prison.

ii
In prison Joseph meets a wine steward and a baker.
The wine steward dreams
and Joseph says: your dream means that
you will be a wine steward again.
The baker dreams
and Joseph says: your dream means that you will be hanged.
And to both dreams
Joseph says: *dream-interpretations are from God,*
and the predictions come true.

And Pharaoh hears of Joseph's dream-interpretation
and Pharaoh makes Joseph ruler over Egypt
and Joseph's brothers do bow to him
and Joseph's dreams come true.

iii
In security Joseph thinks that dreams are promises,
but the promise never takes hold.

Then Joseph sees
that dreams are the signs of changing fortune:
—for good (a return to the world of

wine), or for suffering (a hanging);
only God will say which.

Then dreams speak Truth through Joseph
and his dreams come true.

Because he has learned the heart of
dreams, the core of Truth:
that life is changeable,

that God is the only Master of the change.

———

Inspired largely by Rabbi Alex Israel's
reading of Joseph, and other sources.
Genesis 37:1-42:6

Abe Mezrich

Mikeitz

Then the Lives Will Intertwine

i
Pharaoh dreams
of cows eating cows
and he wakes up
and he goes to sleep
and then he dreams
of corn eating corn.
*

Joseph tells him:
the cows eating cows
and the corn eating corn
all represent
one continuum of years.
Though you woke in between,
your two dreams really are one.
*

Through these dreams
Joseph joins seven years of plenty
with seven years of famine.

Through these dreams
Joseph's many brothers
estranged twenty years
come to meet him now,
the leader in Egypt
far from home.

Through these dreams
Joseph's brothers say finally
we are guilty
for the cruelty they had shown him
when they were young
in that past life.

Abe Mezrich

Through these dreams
Joseph comes to tell his brothers:
All your cruelty was God's plan
to help me save so many.

ii
Life is full of lives
that do not seem to connect.
Some seem unworkable
and some look meaningless
and only later can we say:
Here is what it means.

iii
A people of history,
our lives bear the task
of weaving moments together
past to present
present to future
of saying, It is one dream,
one story
a single life
that God unfolds.

———

Genesis 41:1 – 45:8, 50:20

We Exist Because We Make Each Other Exist

i
Joseph languishes in prison because the wine steward,
freed,
forgets about Joseph.
Out of sight, out of mind.

When the wine steward finally remembers,
he says: *Today I recall my sin.*

He recalls the sin of forgetting Joseph.

And he tells the world about Joseph,
and the world lets Joseph free.

ii
We are so intertwined that sometimes the only way we live
is through each other's memories.
We are so intertwined that sometimes our first obligation
is to simply say:
Yes, I still remember
I do not forget
I still know who you are
you still are.

———

Genesis 41:9-14
In argument with Jean-Paul Sartre

Dreams, Clothes

i
When Joseph is young, in his father's house, and
he dreams and tells his brothers and father of these
dreams, Joseph's father gives him a special coat.

Later Joseph is sent to interpret Pharaoh's dream.
Joseph *changed his garments* to prepare for the
dream-meeting. And after Joseph delivers his
interpretation, Pharaoh *arrayed* Joseph *in garments
of fine linen, and put a gold chain around his neck.*

Dreams and clothes come together.

ii
Dreams and clothes both come from the world of symbol.

Dreams are meanings waiting to be deciphered. Clothes
are patches of cloth that signify, as in uniforms or fashion.

Dreams are a symbol to your internal world.

Clothing is a symbol to the external world.

Dreams and clothing are two parts of a whole.

Do not be surprised that dreams and clothes come together.

iii
Now think of *tzitzit.*

You must put the tzitzit-strings on your clothes.

They are a reminder to follow God, and to not follow *after
your heart and after your eyes, after which you stray.*

Your eyes and your heart are joined.

Your inner and outer world are joined.

Just as dreams and clothes are joined.

If the outer world and the inner world are joined, the tzitzit say,
then the external life must guide the inner life,
the heart and the eyes guided by the stringing of cloth.

You must shape the realm of cloth
to guide the space where dreams live.

————
Genesis 37, 41; Numbers 15:38-41

Abe Mezrich

Carry Mercy to the Earth

i
Jacob says to his sons: *And God Almighty give you mercy.*
Jacob is referring to *mercy* from Joseph.
Joseph, having disguised himself as a tyrant.
Joseph, in the process of exacting vengeance
on his brothers, Jacob's other sons,
who years and years earlier
cast Joseph into a pit to die.

But when Joseph sees his brother Benjamin (his closest
brother), Joseph's *mercy was kindled toward his brother.*

And Joseph tends to his brothers.
And he forgives them.
And he feeds them in famine and gives them land.
And they grow from a family into a people.

ii
Mercy runs from *God Almighty,* down to Joseph.

Divine mercy becomes human mercy.
Divine kindness becomes human kindness.

The nation of Jacob's family is created in that translation.
The people is rooted in that translation.

Gen 43:14, 30

Abe Mezrich

VaYigash

Should we Cut Ourselves Off?

i
God tells Abraham:
Leave your homeland
your birthplace
your father's house,
go to the Land of Israel,
I will make you a great nation there.

There,
Abraham parts ways with his nephew
parts ways with his son
nearly sacrifices his other son upon the altar
becomes the lone Man of God.

ii
Jacob and his whole family
go down to Egypt
reuniting with Jacob's beloved son
—Joseph—
who lives there
who had been estranged from the family
for twenty years.

It will be centuries
before the family returns to the Land.

God tells Jacob:
Do not be afraid to go down to Egypt.
I will make you a great nation there.
And Joseph
your beloved son
will lay his hands over your eyes
when you pass.

iii
Abraham begins *a great nation*
going to the Land.
Jacob begins *a great nation*
leaving it.

God makes us *a great nation*
when we are ready to give up
the people we love
the family around us
to follow God to the Promised Land.

God makes us *a great nation*, too,
when we are ready to put aside that Promise
following the people we love.

———

Genesis Chapter 12:1-2 and through Chapter 23, 46:1-4

Burden of Togetherness

i

When the Cupbearer leaves prison,
he does not speak of Joseph
to the outside world.
Though Joseph has helped him.
Though Joseph has asked the Cupbearer
to tell Joseph's story.

And Joseph languishes in prison.

When the Cupbearer says: *today I recall my sin*
he tells Joseph's story
and Joseph goes free at last.

ii

Joseph, disguised as a tyrant, threatens
to enslave his brother Benjamin.
Their brother Judah says: enslave me instead.

Joseph is so moved he ends the charade.
He ends his acting as a tyrant altogether.

And he is no longer the ruler
who will enslave Benjamin.

I am Joseph, he tells his brothers:
your long lost brother.
You cast me into slavery years ago,
but it was all God's plan:
famine has encompassed the world
but I could save so many.

iii
Take up the burden of the other
and you will find God's plan
that we remember each other
that we burden ourselves for each other
and so free each other
and so go free.

———

Drawn from the ideas of Rav Yaakov Meidan and others.
Genesis 41:9-14, 44:18-45:16, 50:20

Why the Torah is a Story

i
Telling
brings the listener
and the person told about
into one story—
across divides
across lands
across hearts.
*

Here is one example:

ii
Joseph rules Egypt.
He disguises himself from his brothers—
who have hated him,
who have tossed him from home,
from his father.
They come to him now
down from Canaan
to seek bread during famine.
*

But Joseph demands
that they leave their youngest brother,
Benjamin,
in Egypt.
Then the brother Judah describes the whole story:
of the brothers coming to him
from far away
and going back to Canaan
and seeing their father
and returning to Egypt
only for Joseph to demand
that Benjamin stay.
And Judah tells Joseph:

our father's heart will break
there in Canaan
if Benjamin stays
here in Egypt
one more heartbreak
after losing Joseph
(not knowing that he speaks to Joseph)
for this old man to bear.
*

And listening to the story
Joseph *cannot contain himself*
and Joseph says: *I am Joseph.*
And Joseph reconciles with his brothers
and Joseph reunites with his father.

iii
Another example
of uniting through story
is the Torah itself.
Because sometimes God seems far from us.
But hearing the Torah,
studying Torah,
we are reunited with God
into one story,
into one telling
into one book
from across a great distance.

———
With special thanks to my wife Kathi, as always.
Genesis 44:18-Chapter 45

Represents

The tragedy begins with Joseph's coat.
It ends when Judah approaches Joseph face-to-face.
Not what represents us, but who we are.

Genesis 37:3-4, 44:18-Chapter 45

VaYechi

Find the Hidden God

1. Puzzle

Jacob blesses his grandchildren:
let them multiply as fish
in the midst of the land.

Such a strange blessing!

2. Land and Sea

God does not mention *fish*
when He makes the things of the water.
God and the Torah only mention *fish*
when God makes people:
they will *rule* over all things,
they will *rule over the fish of the sea.*

When God rescues Israel from Egypt at the Sea
the Children of Israel *saw the great Hand* of God,
and they believed in God.

We are land dwellers.
Things of the water do not exist for us
until we and they are brought into connection:
until we rule over fish,
until God protects us with His Hand.
Then these things come into view,
and they exist for us.

3. Blessing

To be a fish that thrives on land
is to live that connection
that seems impossibly unapparent
between the world where we exist
and the world beyond—

Abe Mezrich

between the land and the sea,
between our lives
and the Hand of God.

Jacob blesses his grandchildren:
live that hidden connection so firmly
that it becomes you.

————
Genesis Chapter 1, 48:1-15; Exodus Chapter 14

The Past is Not a Promise

i
Jacob flees home, fleeing his brother.
He asks God to *return* him to his father's house—
someday,
when the danger is gone,
when it will be safe.
Then he *lifted up his feet*
and sets off.
*

Decades later
he returns to his father's land
only to leave
living seventeen years in Egypt
dying in Egypt
one-hundred forty seven years old
blessing his twelve sons.
And he gathered his feet
and *was gathered to his nation.*

ii
Young Jacob asks God
for his father's house back,
for his childhood back.
God gives him something else.
God *gathers* Jacob *to his nation,*
not to his father's home.
God makes him an old patriarch
giving blessing,
years past being a child.
*

It is almost a return
but not a return.

iii
God sets us out on a journey
not for us to come back to the same spot
but also not to depart utterly.
We are to lift up our feet
and walk far,
to widen the story:
to make a nation
from a father's home,
fatherhood from childhood,
our time of dependency
into a blessing for others.
*
That is the journey
of a good life.

—————

Genesis 28:20 – 29:1, 47:28, 49:33

A Family is the Heart of the World

i
Before death, Jacob commands his sons
to take his body from Egypt
to the family's burial plot in Canaan.

When Jacob dies, Pharaoh's officers escort Jacob's sons
carrying his body home.

The Canaanites, looking on, say:
Here is a great mourning for Egypt.

ii
A family's loss becomes a nation's loss
becomes a moment on the global stage.

Here is Jacob's final lesson:

Look deep into the global stage
and you will see a family peering back.

____

Inspired by the philosophy of Rav Ezra Bick
Genesis 49:28-33, 50:7-11

Abe Mezrich

Forgiving

i
Joseph tells his brothers
who have cast him off
left him to die in a pit
left him to slavery
left him alone in a strange land
where, amazingly, he achieves great power
rescues a whole region from famine
rescues his brothers and his father from that famine—

Joseph tells these brothers:
I will hold nothing against you.

You thought to do me wrong;
God had in mind that I should go through this
and come to sustain many.

ii
God's plan
in which your life plays a part
in which your tormentors also play a part
is larger than you
larger than your life
larger than your suffering
larger than the cruelty of others.

This knowledge can help you bear much,
can let you forgive.

iii
That is Joseph's message
on the eve of our anguish
at the hands of Egypt
on the way to Redemption.

iv
Perhaps this message
lets Moses say, later:
Do not despise an Egyptian
for you were an immigrant in his land—

see
that we all live in God's plan,

so you can even look at the Egyptian
as a human once again

so your power to forgive is boundless.

––––

Genesis 50:15-20; Deuteronomy 23:8
Inspired in part by Micah Goodman

Abe Mezrich

The Story of Freedom

Shemot Through *Mishpatim*

Abe Mezrich

Shemot

Sending Good

The Egyptians want Jewish babies
so the baby's mother hides him
but you can only hide a baby so long
so she sends him away,
the *good* son,
out into Egypt

where he will become Moses.

Sometimes evil leaves us no choice
but to send good into the world.

––––
Exodus 1-2:3

The Born

God with
- swarms of children, birthed a litter at a time
- rebel mothers, midwives, sisters, daughters
- flowing blood: the source of life
- swarms of frogs, lice, locusts: life

God's fertility
defeats a wicked kingdom

_____

Exodus Chapter 1, 7:14-10:19
Inspired by Mary Douglas

Where is He / Where Are You?

V'ayo
And where is he?
Yitro asked his daughters
when they came home early that day
because Moses had rescued them from the shepherds.

Like the question God had asked Adam
as Adam hid in the Garden:
Ayekah?
Where are you?

Meanwhile in Egypt
the Children of Israel still suffered.

In Yitro's home
Moses married Yitro's daughter
and turned aside to see the burning bush
and God sent Moses back into Egypt
to save His people
because He heard their cries.

Ayekah? / Where are you?
V'ayo / And where is he?
God searches for us
but we do not always hear Him searching.

We must seek each other
until He comes.

––––

Genesis 3:8-9; Exodus 2:16 – Chapter 3

Abe Mezrich

The Wicked are Also in This Story

God commands Moses
to command Pharaoh
to send Israel out
to serve God in the Desert.
*

God could have brought freedom in other ways.
Israel could have won a war against Egypt,
or Israel simply could have walked away.
*

But Israel's freedom is not the story
of strength over enemies
or even the story of Israel standing alone.
Israel's freedom comes in Moses
bringing Pharaoh
to send Israel
to worship God:
in bringing Pharaoh to send Israel to God.
*

When Israel brings God into the deeds
of even the most wicked, then freedom comes.

––––
Exodus 3:15-22

Brotherhood

Often we think: Moses led us from Egypt.

But Moses does not stand before Pharaoh alone.
He stands beside Aaron, his brother.

One leader does not lead us from Egypt.
A brotherhood leads us from Egypt.

Exodus 4:13-16

VaEirah

Instruction

HaShem spoke to both Moses and Aaron
regarding the Israelites
and Pharaoh king of Egypt
to deliver the Israelites from the land of Egypt.

It would seem:

God commands Moses to command Pharaoh to free
and commands Moses to command Israel to become free.

God commands Moses to command
Israel to be ready to be free
and so when Moses commands
Pharaoh to free, Israel will go.

God commands Moses to command Israel to be free
and so even in shackles, we show
the oppressor what he must do.

———

Exodus 6:13

Abe Mezrich

The World We Make

i
God warns Pharaoh:
If you hold on to My people
I will send My Plagues
I will transform Creation.

You are held responsible
for the world I will make.

ii
The first Commandment,
the first Law of our covenant with God,
is not:
I am the Lord Your God Who Created the Universe.

The first Commandment is:
I am the Lord Your God
Who took you from Egypt;
the Lord
Who makes Creation responsible.

iii
We do not become God's because God created the world.
We become God's because we bear
responsibility for God's world.

––––
Exodus 7:1-5, 20:2

What Happens if You See From God's Point of View

i
God said
I will make many
My signs and My wonders
in the Land of Egypt
and this was the start of the Plagues.

God fought for the Children of Israel
through these ten signs and wonders:
these ten symbols.

ii
Symbols are an invitation
to depart from the meanings we give to this world,
to see the world as holding the meaning
someone else has offered us.

iii
At the end of the Plagues
Egypt gleaned the meaning of the Plagues
acceded to the will of God
accepted God's view of the world.

Viewing the world through God's eyes,
Egypt had no choice
but to choose to set others free.

————
Exodus 7:3

What is Power?

i
God smites Egypt
with terrifying hail
fire in ice
thunder
hail that is deadly to animals
destructive to houses
ruinous of crops;
and Pharaoh tells Moses:
I will free Israel,
pray for me
that God ends this hail.
*

Moses tells Pharaoh:
I will lift my hands to God
and He will end this Plague
and you will know
that the land is God's.

ii
If God wanted to show
that the land is His,
wouldn't demolishing the land
have been enough?
But God displays His power
by answering a prayer.
*

Perhaps:
the power to reopen the dialogue
is the power beyond all strengths.

————

Exodus 9:13 - 33
With inspiration from Rav Ezra Bick and Rav Avi Weiss

Abe Mezrich

Bo

No

Moses tells Pharaoh:
God has told us to celebrate
so you must let us go celebrate
and you, too, must send offerings with us
for the celebration to God.

But Pharaoh refuses Moses' demand.

Had Pharaoh said yes,
even he might have had a role to play
in God's service.

If even Pharaoh had a role to play,
think of how many others God might call,
and God might still be calling right now.

Think of how many
God wants to answer Him.

Think of how many
(even you, perhaps)
who will tell God:

No.

‗‗‗‗
Exodus 10:21-29

Who is Most Important?

i
Moses says to Pharaoh:
let us leave Egypt
to hold a celebration to God.

Pharaoh asks:
Who amongst you will go celebrate?

Moses answers:
Our young and our old will go,
our sons and our daughters,
our flocks and our cattle.
All of us.

Pharaoh says:
Not all of you may go.
Only the men may go
to celebrate before God.

ii
Much later we learn:
When you come to the Land,
then the Levites,
the tribe of the priests,
will live among the rest of the people.
And when you *rejoice in all the good that HaShem has given you*,
you must rejoice with *the Levite*.
And you must keep the Sabbath each week
a day of rest
for *you and your son and your daughter*
and your servant
and your animal
and the foreigner who lives in your midst.

For everyone.

iii
Egypt has a citizen nation
and a slave nation
and priests who live on their own separate land.
How could the king of Egypt
tolerate a communal festival?

But God does not want Egypt.
God wants us to celebrate to Him
as many people,
together.

_____

Genesis 47:22; Exodus 10:8-11;
Deuteronomy 5:12-14, 10:9, 26:11
Based on the Ramban and a thought
of Rabbi Menachem Leibtag

Abe Mezrich

Middle Bread

i
There was famine in Canaan and there was no bread
but in Egypt there was bread
so Jacob's sons came to Egypt
and came to stay
in Egypt,
where their grandchildren become enslaved.
*
Israel rose from Egypt
baking matzah:
bread that would not rise,
bread that is not bread.
*
And manna was the bread from God
that Israel ate in the Desert.

ii
Israel eats the bread of Egypt,
and then of God.
Israel belongs to Egypt,
and then to God.
You belong to the one
who gives you bread.

iii
But what of matzah—
no-man's-land,
bread and not bread,
not of Egypt, not from God?
Matzah is the bread of growing up.
*
When you grow up
you come to someone
not as a child

not as a slave
but as a partner,
a groom,
a bride.
*
Before this
you must learn two things:
that you can bake your own bread;
that the bread you feed yourself
is no bread at all.

---

*Genesis Chapter 41 and following; Exodus
12:33-34,39; Exodus 15:24-36*

Abe Mezrich

What We Discover

Because the woman is made from the man,
the man said *etzem* of my *etzem* – *bone of my
bone, self of my self* – when he saw her.

Because she is of his bone, of his *etzem*, a man
will grow up and go to his wife and *cleave to his
wife and they will be as one* basar – *one flesh.*

On Passover we eat of the *basar*–the *meat*, the
same word as *flesh*—of the Passover lamb.

On Passover we may not break a single
bone—a single *etzem*—of the lamb.

On Passover we eat the Passover lamb *by family.*

In Creation we learned to find our self in another.

In freedom we learned that the self is unbreakable.

Both are how we find each other, join together,
undoing all the loneliness of the world.

———

Genesis 2:18-24; Exodus Chapter 12

Quarantine Seder

None of you shall go outside the door of his house until
morning.
—Exodus 12:22

It went like this: All of them in their own homes,
at their own tables.
Outside was the danger in the darkness.
And then the next home, the next family inside.

They knew about the danger all around them.
They knew about the darkness.
They knew, also, about each other between the darkness.

All that time before they had toiled together,
but it did not make them a nation yet.

Now they were one.

BeShalach

Salvation

God tells Moses,
Why do you cry out to Me?
Move into the unpassable water.

& when the people do,

God splits the Sea
into a miracle.

Sometimes you cry out for help
but sometimes God wants, instead,
for you to walk so deep into your own waters
that you force His Hand.

‎‎‎———

Exodus Chapter 14

What Do You Own?

i
God tells Pharaoh to send Israel from Egypt
but Pharaoh refuses.
God tells Moses:
Let Aaron cast a stick upon the river
and I will turn the river to blood.

The water becomes blood
and the river fish die
and the river goes rancid
and Egypt cannot drink from it.

ii
And Israel leaves Egypt
and comes to the desert
and the people find water
but the water is bitter.

God shows Moses a tree
to take and cast into the water
and Moses casts the tree into the water
and the water becomes sweet.

iii
Egypt may have a good river
and Israel may have bitter water
but none of this needs to matter:

It is God Who decides
which water is drinkable
which water is not.
It is God who decides
what is salty

what is bitter
what could be sweet.

————

Exodus 7:19-24, 15:22-25

Abe Mezrich

Each One Must Bear Witness

i

The Children of Israel murmured in the Desert
against Moses and against Aaron:

Would we had died…in Egypt
when we sat by the pots of meat
and when we ate our fill of bread
and now you have brought us out
into this Desert
to kill this whole assembly with hunger.

Then God sends the people manna
—nourishment for their Desert life.

And when God promises He will provide food,
the Presence of HaShem appeared before the people.

ii
These people have watched God deliver the Ten Plagues.
They have seen God split open the sea,
and drown the Egyptian army in it.
They have sung: *Sing to HaShem, for He has triumphed.*

But these are lofty things.
These are national things.
Hunger is a personal matter.

iii
God says: Everyone must gather manna
according to his own appetite,
for himself and for *those in his tent.*

So everyone's own family encounters God.
And everyone's own hunger has its encounter with God.

God says: I am the God
Who even tends to each one of you.

It is in this relationship
they witness *the Presence of HaShem.*

____

Exodus 15:1, 16:2-3,10,16

Units

God sends Manna:
a unit
for each person
for each day—
& no more.

Each person is complete & nourished by God.
Each day is complete & nourished by God.

_____

Exodus 16:4-30

Abe Mezrich

Yitro

Together (I)

i
Moses goes out to the desert alone
to the mountain alone
and must turn to the bush
to encounter God there.

ii
The people go to that desert together
to that mountain together
and when they are together
they do not need to happen upon God.
He comes down
to all of them.

____

Exodus 3:1-12, Chapters 19-20

Abe Mezrich

How Does My Small Life Matter?

i
God says:
Remember the Sabbath day. Work for six days
and on the seventh you shall rest
because God worked for six days
and on the seventh He rested.
*

But it is unclear what we must *remember*:
if we must remember God's rest,
or we must simply recall
that we must rest each week
and God's long-ago rest
is only background
for what we do now,
what we remember now.

ii
This lack of clarity
this permeable line
between your week and God's
points to how your week
is part of God's week:
how within the long coursing
endless history
of all of God's work,
since the beginning of Time,
your week is there.

iii
And to delve deeply into your week
to become deeply aware of your week
to *remember* your week
is to know this,
is to *remember* this:

that all along your weeks have been holy,
that all along your life has been holy,
that all that you've lived,
day in and day out
week in and week out
has been tied to God.

———

Exodus 20:8-11

Abe Mezrich

Commandments

Commandment 2

Have no idols:
images to worship
of the things of the heavens
& of the earth
& of the waters.

Commandment 4

Keep the Sabbath
as God did.

Together

Do not seek out gods.
Be like God.

Exodus 20:1-11
Based on ideas of Rav Amital and Yonatan Grossman

Together (II)

Moses says:
soon God will come to the Mountain,
now you must prepare.
Let no man go near a woman.

But when Moses is up on the mountain
there with God,
the men snatch earrings from their wives
and sons and daughters.
They make the Golden Calf from those earrings
and God nearly departs.

After God forgives them,
the people make His Tent
and the men come with the women
—the *men came on the women*, the text literally says—
bringing jewels and goods and craftwork
to build the holy place.
And God comes down:

not down to the mountain
but much lower,

to the Tent the men and women have built,

to God's home
they have made together.

____

Exodus 19:1-15, 32:1-6

Abe Mezrich

Justice is a Family Reunion

Yitro returns with his daughter & Moses' children
& offers a judicial system for all Israel

the father and the mother
and the children come back
the fathers made fathers again
the children may be loved again
justice, says the father throughout the land
justice, say the children throughout the land

i ask you what is justice first & foremost
a means to punish
or simply to say My children My children

————

Exodus Chapter 18

After Lucille Clifton

And Then God Revealed

When God comes to us
let husbands and wives be apart
so they will be ready.

When God comes to us
let the mountain be bordered off
so no one rushes up
to find the heights.

When God comes to us
let it be in a desert:
Not where we come from
and not where we will be,
but where it is no one's country
and no one's true home.

When God comes to us
let it be black fire
on white fire,
the light of absence on absence.

When God comes to us
let the emptiness have its space
and let it be filled with the memory we allow ourselves
and the hope we allow ourselves
that is like the hope you could see in the void
when the universe began.

In that space
in that emptiness
in that quiet
let us invite God.

--
Exodus Chapter 19

Abe Mezrich

Mishpatim

What is Freedom?

i
After six years of service
the slave goes free.

But the slave may still say:
I love my master
I love my wife
       that my master has given me
I love the children
       that this wife has given me

and he may choose to stay a slave
with his beloved master
with his beloved wife
with their beloved children.

ii
Freedom is the freedom to go
freedom is also the freedom
to make the so-hard choice
to stay with those whom you love.

————

Exodus 21:1-6

Abe Mezrich

What is Community?

a life for a life
an eye for an eye
a tooth for a tooth
a hand for a hand
a foot for a foot
a burn for a burn
a wound for a wound
a bruise for a bruise

Your life and your neighbor's life
your eye and your neighbor's eye
your tooth and your neighbor's tooth
your hand and your neighbor's hand
are utterly linked
they are two parts of a whole
you cannot hurt someone else
without feeling his pain.

––––

Exodus 21:23-25

Rest

1.
If the ox gores & kills, kill it by stoning.

2.
Rest on Sabbath so your ox, too, may rest.

3.
Even the dangerous one deserves rest.
Even the ox has his day with God.

———
Exodus 21: 28-32, 23:12

Words for a Dazzling Firmament

i

Moses *told the people*
the *words of HaShem,*

read to them aloud
from *the Book of the Covenant.*

And *the people saw the God of Israel*
and below His *feet*
was like sapphire brick pavement.

This all happened
as we accepted God's Law.

ii

VaYisaper	וַיְסַפֵּר	and he told
Sepher	סֵפֶר	book
Sapir	סַפִּיר	sapphire

each new layer
a continuation of the last,

each new layer
a solidification of the last:

From God's words
       Moses fashioned a telling
and from a telling a book
       to hold and to read from
and from a book

brickwork
like jewels the color of the sky.

iii
This is what happens
as we bring God's Law
onto the earth

each stage of our accepting
something more concrete
something more of the earth

until we reach
a holiness so concrete
God Himself
will lay His feet there.

—

Exodus 24:3-10

Acknowledgements

To Jay Michaelson for believing that I should get my writing out there all those years ago. To Larry Yudelson for bringing me in to an amazing Jewish Poetry Project which is transforming Jewish language as we speak. To Joey Yudelson for all his care and input on *Between the Mountain and the Land Lies the Lesson*. To Julia Knobloch for bringing her deep knowledge of craft to help make *Words for a Dazzling Firmament* a better book. To Kathi for helping me understand what I'm trying to say, and for being a part of what I want to say. To HaShem for bringing all of these people into my life, and for bringing words into my life, and for helping me place my words into this world.

Abe Mezrich

About Abe Mezrich

Abe Mezrich wants to know what our sacred texts say about our world right now. Sometimes he writes down his answers to those questions. His writing, some featured (sometimes in edited form) in this book, has appeared in outlets including *929*, *The Forward*, *The Los Angeles Jewish Journal*, *Lehrhaus*, *Tablet*, *The New York Jewish Week*, *The Times of Israel*, and *Zeek*. His prior books, *The House at the Center of the World: Poetic Midrash on Sacred Space* and *Between the Mountain and the Land Lies the Lesson: Poetic Midrash on Sacred Community*, are also available through Ben Yehuda Press. He lives with his wife Kathi and their three children. Learn more at www.abemezrich.com.

The Jewish Poetry Project

jpoetry.us

Ben Yehuda Press

From the Coffee House of Jewish Dreamers: Poems of Wonder and Wandering and the Weekly Torah Portion by Isidore Century

"Isidore Century is a wonderful poet. His poems are funny, deeply observed, without pretension." – *The Jewish Week*

The House at the Center of the World: Poetic Midrash on Sacred Space by Abe Mezrich

"Direct and accessible, Mezrich's midrashic poems often tease profound meaning out of his chosen Torah texts. These poems remind us that our Creator is forgiving, that the spiritual and physical can inform one another, and that the supernatural can be carried into the everyday."
—Yehoshua November, author of *God's Optimism*

we who desire:
Poems and Torah riffs by Sue Swartz

"Sue Swartz does magnificent acrobatics with the Torah. She takes the English that's become staid and boring, and adds something that's new and strange and exciting. These are poems that leave a taste in your mouth, and you walk away from them thinking, what did I just read? Oh, yeah. It's the Bible."
—Matthue Roth, author, *Yom Kippur A Go-Go*

Open My Lips: Prayers and Poems
by Rachel Barenblat

"Barenblat's God is a personal God—one who lets her cry on His shoulder, and who rocks her like a colicky baby. These poems bridge the gap between the ineffable and the human. This collection will bring comfort to those with a religion of their own, as well as those seeking a relationship with some kind of higher power."
—Satya Robyn, author, *The Most Beautiful Thing*

Words for Blessing the World: Poems in Hebrew and English by Herbert J. Levine

"These writings express a profoundly earth-based theology in a language that is clear and comprehensible. These are works to study and learn from."
—Rodger Kamenetz, author, *The Jew in the Lotus*

Shiva Moon: Poems by Maxine Silverman

"The poems, deeply felt, are spare, spoken in a quiet but compelling voice, as if we were listening in to her inner life. This book is a precious record of the transformation saying Kaddish can bring."
—Howard Schwartz, author, *The Library of Dreams*

is: heretical Jewish blessings and poems by Yaakov Moshe (Jay Michaelson)

"Finally, Torah that speaks to and through the lives we are actually living: expanding the tent of holiness to embrace what has been cast out, elevating what has been kept down, advancing what has been held back, reveling in questions, revealing contradictions."
—Eden Pearlstein, aka eprhyme

Texts to the Holy: Poems
by Rachel Barenblat

"These poems are remarkable, radiating a love of God that is full bodied, innocent, raw, pulsating, hot, drunk. I can hardly fathom their faith but am grateful for the vistas they open. I will sit with them, and invite you to do the same."
—Merle Feld, author of *A Spiritual Life*

The Sabbath Bee: Love Songs to Shabbat
by Wilhelmina Gottschalk

"Torah, say our sages, has seventy faces. As these prose poems reveal, so too does Shabbat. Here we meet Shabbat as familiar housemate, as the child whose presence transforms a family, as a spreading tree, as an annoying friend who insists on being celebrated, as a woman, as a man, as a bee, as the ocean."
—Rachel Barenblat, author, *The Velveteen Rabbi's Haggadah*

All the Holes Line Up: Poems and Translations
by Zackary Sholem Berger

"Spare and precise, Berger's poems gaze unflinchingly at—but also celebrate—human imperfection in its many forms. And what a delight that Berger also includes in this collection a handful of his resonant translations of some of the great Yiddish poets." —Yehoshua November, author of *God's Optimism* and *Two World Exist*

How to Bless the New Moon: The Priestess Paths Cycle and Other Poems for Queens
by Rachel Kann

"To read Rachel Kann's poems is to be confronted with the possibility that you, too, are prophet and beloved, touched by forces far beyond your mundane knowing. So, dear reader, enter into the 'perfumed forcefield' of these words—they are healing and transformative."
—Rabbi Jill Hammer, co-author of *The Hebrew Priestess*

Into My Garden
by David Caplan

"The beauty of Caplan's book is that it is not polemical. It does not set out to win an argument or ask you whether you've put your tefillin on today. These gentle poems invite the reader into one person's profound, ambiguous religious experience."
— *The Jewish Review of Books*

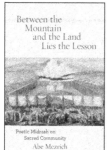

Between the Mountain and the Land is the Lesson: Poetic Midrash on Sacred Community
by Abe Mezrich

"Abe Mezrich cuts straight back to the roots of the Midrashic tradition, sermonizing as a poet, rather than idealogue. Best of all, Abe knows how to ask questions and avoid the obvious answers."
—Jake Marmer, author, *Jazz Talmud*

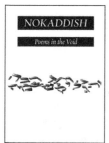

NOKADDISH: Poems in the Void
by Hanoch Guy Kaner

"A subversive, midrashic play with meanings–specifically Jewish meanings, and then the reversal and negation of these meanings."
—Robert G. Margolis

An Added Soul: Poems for a New Old Religion
by Herbert Levine

"These poems are remarkable, radiating a love of God that is full bodied, innocent, raw, pulsating, hot, drunk. I can hardly fathom their faith but am grateful for the vistas they open. I will sit with them, and invite you to do the same."
—Merle Feld, author of *A Spiritual Life*.

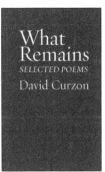

What Remains
by David Curzon

"Aphoristic, ekphrastic, and precise revelations animate WHAT
REMAINS. In his stunning rewriting of Psalm 1 and other
biblical passages, Curzon shows himself to be a fabricator,
a collector, and an heir to the literature, arts, and wisdom
traditions of the planet."
—Alicia Ostriker, author of *The Volcano and After*

The Shortest Skirt in Shul
by Sass Oron

"These poems exuberantly explore gender, Torah, the masks we
wear, and the way our bodies (and the ways we wear them) at
once threaten stable narratives, and offer the kind of liberation
that saves our lives."
—Alicia Jo Rabins, author of *Divinity School*, composer of *Girls
In Trouble*

Walking Triptychs
by Ilya Gutner

These are poems from when I walked about Shanghai and
thought about the meaning of the Holocaust.

Book of Failed Salvation
by Julia Knobloch

"These beautiful poems express a tender longing for spiritual,
physical, and emotional connection. They detail a life in
movement—across distances, faith, love, and doubt."
—David Caplan, author, *Into My Garden*

Daily Blessings: Poems on Tractate Berakhot
by Hillel Broder

"Hillel Broder does not just write poetry about the Talmud; he also draws out the Talmud's poetry, finding lyricism amidst legality and re-setting the Talmud's rich images like precious gems in end-stopped lines of verse."
—Ilana Kurshan, author of *If All the Seas Were Ink*

The Missing Jew: Poems 1976-2022
by Rodger Kamenetz

"How does Rodger Kamenetz manage to have so singular a voice and at the same time precisely encapsulate the world view of an entire generation (also mine) of text-hungry American Jews born in the middle of the twentieth century?"
—Jacqueline Osherow, author, *Ultimatum from Paradise* and *My Lookalike at the Krishna Temple: Poems*

The Red Door: A dark fairy tale told in poems
by Shawn Harris

"THE RED DOOR, like its poet author Shawn C. Harris, transcends genres and identities. It is an exploration in crossing worlds. It brings together poetry and story telling, imagery and life events, spirit and body, the real and the fantastic, Jewish past and Jewish present, to spin one tale."
—Einat Wilf, author, *The War of Return*

The Matter of Families
by Robert Deluty

"Robert Deluty's career-spanning collection of New and Selected poems captures the essence of his work: the power of love, joy, and connection, all tied together with the poet's glorious sense of humor. This book is Deluty's masterpiece."
—Richard M. Berlin, M.D., author of *Freud on My Couch*

CPSIA information can be obtained
at www.ICGtesting.com
Printed in the USA
BVHW050302140922
646955BV00002B/105